Kevin Kiely was born in 1953 in Warrenpoint, Co. Down. He has lived, worked and studied in England, Spain and the United States. He is the author of two novels, *Quintesse* (St. Martin's Press, 1982) and *Mere Mortals* (Poolbeg Press, 1986). A poetry pamphlet, *Plainchant for a Sundering* (Lapwing Press) appeared in 2001. A dramatist as well as a poet, two of his plays for radio have been broadcast by RTE, *Multiple Indiscretions* and *Children of No Importance*. He is the recipient of six Arts Council Bursary Awards in Literature and is Honorary Fellow-in-Writing at the University of Iowa. Currently Assistant Editor of *Books Ireland*, he is completing a biography of Francis Stuart and a series of novels for children.

By the same author

Fiction
Quintesse
Mere Mortals

Drama
Multiple Indiscretions
Children of No Importance

BREAKFAST WITH SYLVIA

BREAKFAST WITH SYLVIA

KEVIN KIELY

LAGAN PRESS
BELFAST
2005

Acknowledgements

Many of the following have been published in: *Acumen*, *Adrift* (New York), *Anvil*, *The Belle*, *The Black Mountain Review*, *Burning Bush*, *Chapman* (Scotland), *Cork Literary Review*, *Criterion*, *Crystal*, *Cyphers*, *The Democrat Arts Page*, *The Edinburgh Review*, *Foolscap* (London), *Fortnight*, *InCognito*, *The Literary Review* (NJ), *The Mayo News*, *Oasis* (London), *Other Poetry*, *Poetry Ireland Review*, *Riposte*, *The Salmon*, *The Shop*, *Southword*, *Storm* (Scotland), *Touchstone* (UK).

Published by
Lagan Press
Unit 11
1A Bryson Street
Belfast BT5 4ES
e-mail: lagan-press@e-books.org.uk
web: lagan-press.org.uk

arts
council
of Northern Ireland

ISBN: 1 904652 17 4
Author: Kiely, Kevin
Title: Breakfast with Sylvia
2005

Set in Sabon
Design: December
Printed by Easyprint, Belfast

Contents

Shakespeare & Co.

George rules from his riverside bookshop
four storeys high along rue de la Bûcherie
proudly claiming Walt Whitman as his ancestor—
shelf after laden-shelf rising like wine racks in the city
the roving eye can soft focus anywhere—a Faber
translation of *Laments* by Jan Kochanowski

for free accommodation upstairs—you must read
    a book a day
tend the shop now and then, live on pancakes
chocolate croissants or whatever your budget will allow—
two Londoners outside the kitchen on clarinet and fiddle
play Jazz Suite No. 2 (Shostakovich)

George seems oblivious among the backpacked
    youth at table
facing a cracked plate
a fork with sugar on the prongs and a pot of honey (*miel*)
as he plans another week's rota
for this Shangri-la
where the living and the dead
confront each other

Overnight

The funicular creaks and crunches against the rails
up and up the mountain slope
the sheer height and fall to instant death
and our laughing high on the summit

the *Gasthaus* served soup
olives, bread, sweet potatoes, spiced pork
beer in phial-like glasses
the sharp syrup tang of it through froth

would we stay the night under the eaves?
a stair railing beside our bed
and through the open window
stars and the dark weave of the nightsky
a chill breeze mixed with the pine smell

you gave off heat—an Eve woman
under the wooden roof as I dozed towards sleep
one hand resting on your belly
we woke and snuggled into each other's arms
during birdcalls

pans rattled downstairs in the kitchen
the smell of baking bread and breakfast cooking
so close the crackle seemed near our teeth
as we swayed in pleasure, mouths like bitten apples
riven bodies shocked releasing the fears of life
before a bath

Siren

You Siren. Glazed and tired with your
chocolate biscuit and papercup of tea
dreaming through the glass partition
sometimes violent and erotic thoughts
dashed by sunlight brighter than neon
as you type on the grey keys
before the winking computer screen
behind the blinking photocopiers.

How cynically the waves break far away
from your pricey and poky apartment
later you go to the basement clubs
with their Homeric and glitzy names
often bitter and will only talk
where the horizons meet in common bondage:
jobs pay holidays rent taxes
how do you transcend it?

What's the word for it
in a word? A big word
beaten out of sense by overuse in ads
on the box, press, magazines and movies
the glimpsed vivid blue only visible
somewhere in your interior apartment

So that as you climb three flights and pause
by the scruffy chaise longue
the feeling is not quite the core and nugget
chain and anchor. Perhaps after a drenching shower
as your hand touches your teeth for a moment
and you lean against the wall inside at last
though could have stayed out to soaking point
that moment may indicate its filigree

Remember the confectionery shop
where in the window the golden honey
from a tap ever rushing into snowy sugar
shot with sunlight when the clouds moved
after the boom and whistle of a jet
low across the city
its shadow flitting along
the highrise offices

Your white dress on the whiter chair
some enormous apple petal blown onto a snowfall
a storm in your head turns over chairs
knocks the geranium from the mantel
leaving the broken stem and earth and orange pot
on the black stained board floor, still life study
of disgust. Anyway you liked the present
inside the cover I wrote: 'Poets lie too much'
(Nietzsche)

Years later and oft upon an afternoon
quick glance outside to the electric pylons
in brighter silver than mist silver
like elfin Eiffel towers here in this Irish city
gloomy and moaning *tous les moans*
then a breath felt in a room
a presence in a bar
when the glass is stood on the marble finally and full
and recall that first scenery view of the Pyrenees
with morning moon a semi-circular brush stroke
a bronze sickle blade
above the snow capped pyramidical Pyrenees.

Breakfast with Sylvia Plath

I

In Café Insomnia, anaemic sunlight
traffic outside
the rain-flecked picture window
sizzling bacon, eggs wide eyed
frying on the gas

the face by turns, almond pale and fire bright
a streak of lip paint on the brilliant teeth
she eyes the menu in a seething force-nine rage
her conversation post modern in its tangled sense

... bad dreams about a hare
run over by a Morris estate wagon
driven by Edward Hughes
his *Meinkampf* look (his cock runneth over)
the car with a split screen
two steering wheels, one for her father, Otto
who skinned a rat in front of his students
cooked, and ate it

I won't mention that awful weevil of a woman
I will never speak to God again

Edward Hughes should have
scratched on my tombstone:
it was a fight to the death
she or I
had to die
something of me died with her.

II

Sivvy ordered
from the tightly clenched menu
pointing with a bandaged thumb

two glasses of milk and bread
nothing else, thank you
the waitress moved off

other tables were served hot food
but the beekeeper's daughter
shrill in convulsive chatter
shaken through the air
crackling with blue light
her bones almost wrenched from the muscles
as if, at any moment the jelly would spill out

fingered a piece of bread,
but did not eat, her milk untouched
then another mood swing:
I lost an overcoat and keys
but I had a spare set—
I sucked but not for long
the sweet and sickly atmosphere
of 23 Fitzroy Road, London NW1

on the wall
outside the front door
a blue plaque to W.B. Yeats
which I knew
was mine too
when I became Christ and Keats

place a dozen yellow roses
in the empty oven, door open
towel inside for a pillow

O my children

The Inistiogue Mood

You are in my arms
at a wedding party in the marquee
waltzing and lepping to bluegrass and jazz
amongst the hundred guests
cameras digital and flash
round tables bottles glasses ashtrays

the taxi to the guesthouse in the freezing early hours
our starry night view
the murky river
sloshing past under moonlight
beyond the bridge coloured lights
proclaim the festive season
veils of penlight drip from eaves
of the shut pub and restaurant

what hangs in the scales as you unveil
from your black and purple outfit
first off the glinting silver of the waistband
what chains fasten you from yourself—
Cleopatra of the Nore
chains of flowers, my winter rose
in what mood are you now—

our talk wanders through the events
of the evening, as far as the bipolar regions
of desiccated thought washed in wine
the ice in your cold eyes sparkles
in the lamplight

I feel I must give you everything
but I was always on for the long haul
why are you such a task mistress
from whom I steal thunder and sunshine
to soar and plunge, as you enter the duvet

The Unattainable

My wife's asleep with the youngest beside her
the older two with schoolbags ready for another day
there aren't many photos of you in the album.
Trucks sped past to the city dump this morning
your office put me through but I clicked off
the grey birds came inland from the cold sea.
What is there in the drugs of our stolen
conversations, walking detours to face the others
all too soon, hasty goodbyes—a greeting card
a Gershwin cassette. After a compulsory shower
my eyes rimmed in red, daydreams continue
you walk from summergreen trees as only you can
smiling in diaphanous silk sucking my life out
bringing a kind of buttoned up death
with concealed purpose, complete mystery
dazzling and perhaps more longed for
the sensual can fructify the spiritual
the expense of sending invisible roses
is a crazy time until some future in actuality.
Come day go day, domestic duty, a slave to scribbling
a doctor of despair, suburban hostage
with no ransom expected? Empty wine bottle.
dried flowers for the winter. Sunday papers
for the week. Is this an overstatement,
the woman in white can make and break you.

With a Lot of Help from Ovid

Ovid advises find a fatal flaw.
She may have something lacking in her lips
hard to see where she breaks beauty's law
there is no imperfection in her hips
she walks and smokes, her breath smells fine
and laughing tilts but never topples
mixes metaphor and with ease the wine,
never saw such plump delicious apples
she reads a lot, prefers the screen
and tells her stories in a thin disguise
with money she is frugal, perhaps mean
chin apart, what hair, what face, what eyes
her bathroom displays in a glass case
hollow skeleton of a cat's face.

Rue de la Vielle Lanterne, Paris

Actress goddess Jenny Colon's memory
of a four poster bed sent to her door
—his bad move in that failed seduction.
Dr Blanche among the goose-pimpled inmates
in iced-water baths at the asylum
not surprised at the wino-poet's suicide
dangling from window bars at the Doss
infrequent poems in short lived journals

Lobster on a dog leash, unsure movements
of head and limbs like its keeper's protest
it will be my last madness to believe
myself a poet : criticism will cure me of it
Poems unlocked nervous de Nerval's vision
beyond language fantasy identity

Before It Gets dark

How many days until I see you again ...
You were everywhere beside me on the flow
in the woods and paths between grass
through distant reeds, the lake
with a sunstripe across it
tinting leaves and bark of still trees
a branching elbow out of ivy
above flowers drowning sungold
charcoal firs promise nightfall
lemon moon caught in branches
wrist of a V-branch leans but not aimlessly
bird on the weather vane
flitting south east north west
a crossroads to sleep, naming you
yardlights, mercury irises of eyes
every noise could be your knock
when will your feet be heard on the gravel
and you framed in the wingèd-glass
window of the door before I open

To Conjure Up

I went absent leaving you for Chicago
the hotel became a hospital
I signed my committal form at reception

at the Sears Tower in the elevator,
a silver walled room, powered by jet engines
thrust me with strangers to the 110th floor

from this height through the windows—the lights
in the towers of the city, the moving lights
of traffic and streetlights still, far below.

a snowy cloud passed across the window, dimming
the scene of the black and the lights and the towers
with you missing I could only conjure you up.
and then I said: I will give you all of this city

below us from this mad height if you bow down
and adore me. I bow down and adore you by the waters
of Lake Michigan breaking and breaking in waves
without salt

and she said: I will bow down and adore you.
so I gave her the city
with pleasure I gave her the city of Chicago

Thank You, Jakob Boehme

The glare of this compact brilliance stings the eyes
real Christmas card scenery
brave kids sculpt sling and slide
flakes melt in the hand
fleece falling that way
why this colour and highlighter of forms
when a mere cooling of vapour
like rain does rain's work
without the spectacular metaphorical gesture
in these providential atoms
boil them and the water is dirty
milk lily lyric
powered to destroy and paralyse
without signing leaves its signature
ceaseless crystals of white light
wax drops from the white candle of the world
the light of the world

Yesterday She Read Coleridge to Me

In the car after communion over the phone
Speeding between flood river, tar road and
Tracts of trees honeyed in morning light,
Fast rewind to repeat the music on cassette,
Along the narrow hill-road to Luttrell castle
A pheasant scrambles up a ditch—a shock
Of colour like the rainbow I cling to
And further on, a tangle of sticks in sunglow
Become a stag's head. You tell me to sprinkle them
With gold dust and bring them to life.
Near you is such life
And away from you such death, and death
Because of you, appears joyful when I soar
Above the valley, heaving out of the body
Into the truer essence, instantaneously falling
Rising and moving in many directions
On the newer zone, with newer senses
New colours, awesome shapes to the sight
After traversing a Milky Way of white light
At such speed, in such a short time.

That is as much as I imagined
On this side of paradise
When the train thundered between waiting cars
At the level crossing of Coolmine station
My eyes drowned getting to a lay-by.
Your shaping flame which burns me, Jesus of women
Coming through a wall panel onto the dancefloor
Outshining your jewels
Observing from a diethylamide haze
Yet introspective.
Give me this day my daily acid burning
From synapse to synapse
Keeping the cellular stairs dusted.

I want to tell you everything that can be said
O matchless one, smoking or non-smoking?
Caressing the music and the air
Laughing at yourself for serious steps
Then serious faced at hanging loose
Stiffening every mudra, reeling into fulsomeness
The bacchanal when opaque talk is broken
Into playful inoffensive chunks of nonsense
With other layers of meaning
When you're above, casting out what is below
When you're the nightsky, city lights
As far as thought can reach
The texture of all minds and their actions
In short, I find god in you
And fuck it all, ease, a feast of hashish
And what might be. Let's go to the garden
Of delightful play among the wine fountains
And feast near the maze of shops and streets
Music and company, last night's fun
The moments by the weir when a bus
Passed beyond the high wall and your
Hand rested on my shoulder and we talked
Much closer than we stood face to face
As if no before and after would succeed
That time emblazoned in some forever.
Believe in my imaginary altar to you
Out there in the rambling city
Where rainbows girder the sky
After rain, and sun shafts the helices
And lozenges of the heavenly dome.
Surely you whose veins are in flood
of which the greater essence is of
Some imperishable spark
Sleep well in the mountains
But come home to the valley soon and steel
The will with plans and schemes

Break in a passionate phrase
'How is every tiny particle of you tonight?'
I am fine thinking of you tonight
The full moon's a photo developing its face
And long to hear you
And sit across from you

When It's Over
old sonnet form

I've lost you then or is it you've lost me
and once more on the newsfront what a mess
I did, you did go deep we both felt free
it's wiser not to damn but somehow bless
the will's the way go onwards, all that stuff
life's beyond belief and might have been
not long now you know and that's no bluff
who'll keep me clear, unseen and seen
how far, how far and then how soon it's done
after the feast, the vinegar until
new gossip and in the memory of two or one
cool reason, lessens the bitter pill
It's nice to keep in touch and have a friend
Forget, look up, remember there's an end

Night and Morning

In the garden of life with rats and snakes
and sagging trees of laden fruit
and vines burnt dark and bright for bottling
she pours for him
before the table is stripped
and he pours for her
in the gallery of faces
where murals depicting night and morning
change to windows in the walls

she goes through cave-like halls
up steps half-lit in the sinking city
fountains of liquid silver slicing light
flesh is sexy framed in taxi glass
they are sipping each other's wine

and clear
in daylight the weir
cleansing their minds
setting last night
in a new morning song

Arts Festival

Across at the pub some local Michelangelo
has muralised you in a suit on cloud nine
a sort of Sligo in Heaven
executed with naive lumps of paint

The journalist, the peacock scholar, the piss artist
made their carnival on high stools
about your moved bones in happy Drumcliffe
Willie, the most holy last lovely Romantic
the skipper at home his spirit soaring

Indeed I felt no need to curse your bones
near the upturned huge boat of Bulben
or your epitaph from Shakespeare's Timon
festive ghost—cast a cold eye on poetry.

Lunatic Lover

Ask not less than everything when the pulse is quick
the soft staring eyes of you coiling dusky hair
come high and higher, then a key-click
away from the hell of huge crates marked 'despair'
in mid-sentence you change voice
I see a place to put down, I may land near
this runway on the world, the choice
of melodious sphere after sphere
the pulsating of every star, city and country
I don't burn in fear or terror
alive beyond faith, hope or expectation
no depth of depth of depth shall break me
the river of ink, the park, and us
and background music from Sibelius

Who's Afraid of Ezra Pound?

Hang it all? They locked you in a cage at Pisa
then twelve years in St Elizabeth's for treason
never madder than Dante or Cavalcanti
hunting usury through twenty centuries
with chunks of rhetoric in the *Cantos*
and a few more cant than canto
Shark's teeth of your form lit in sylvan igneousness
from *illuminatio coitu* to Browning trochees
victim of some unfaithful establishment brochures
Surgeon-critic castigating hackneyed drivel
amongst the printing glut and printmania
leading your paideuma towards kulchurality
Your rancour was not always creative
Or did the rancour consume you?

Requiem for Kurt Cobain

Sleep is fitful and almost free
the overpass for a roof
rain is welcome on a hurt face
living in walless Seattle
beware of what you ask for
and lose nirvana for fame
dollars cast out real joy
and dull the guitar's gear shift
until you break the pain barrier
in 'Lithium'
('light my candles in a daze 'cos I found God')

Recurring dreams of clawing bubbles
down to the sand beneath the seaswell
to the rocks that sink a bad marriage
a daughter's voice singing in your ears

at the end of the quest you find
a rifle drained the fever from your mind

Skimming Sam Beckett

with delicate linguistic flair
he makes bleak beauty of despair
raising the spirits from deep
stupor, thrown in the usual heap
imagining fear anxiety pain
the senses unite to conspire again
since every thought is real
with little pretence to feel
once in—it seems unending
not seems—it is unending
voice given to the dumb
descent when the mind grows numb
unsuitable life ill-fitting
the flails and hollows
of guillotine-laughter knitting
lines for an irish gallows
art-rescue for lessness
more or less

Missing You Already

Cannot take in the magazine article
illustrated—showing desert around flowering cacti
the shut-down railway, airport, road
glaring burnt sand whiter than salt

Your crumpled photograph from sweaty fingers
in my pocket. *Maid of Mann* that staggers and ploughs
the drills of foam, pushes
drags our cargo across the Irish sea
trucks, buses and other tons of metal
with each roll of water that has us leaning
sideways then pitching back
as I imagine the ferry load of screaming tourists
luggage, vehicles capsizing

Two *Solian* tablets—on the packet:
'not to be taken with alcohol'—along with a beer.
I want to be a Jolly Roger
ship-shape but not seasick
I must avoid thoughts of falling
emotionally raw as the corridors heave and creak
become hilly and break up every stroll
the clock in the bar is a noose
I should clutch the wheel of it
and steer at high speed until I stop by gravel
and open-gates (hours away yet) ring the doorbell
find out where you are

Instead crazy scenes flit into the mind:
and conflicting messages on imagination's e-mail
the only magic I possess is the photograph
I stare at it in a blur and animate your face

50

A Few Chords for Lar Cassidy

'I'll sing a psalm as I watch it burn
And the ashes I'll keep in a one-handled urn.'
                    —James Joyce, *Gas from a Burner*

The cremation at Glasnevin
Had a few laughs amidst the gloom
Some wag said—'a huge mob
for an Art's Council funeral!'
But your ashes were released
from a clifftop at Dungloe
into the Atlantic
a gale arose taking them
and the sun beamed bright
as your salt blessed the sea.

We had only a few disputes
about poets, critics and the scene—
let-outs at 'Carrigdoon' in Dungloe
that broke up at dawn and began again
with afternoon breakfast and more jazz
for a soundtrack. The house full of people
those wild carefree summers.
Or back east the leisure of late night walks
around Cornelscourt, Carrickmines
Knocksinna. Parties with dope and wine.
Us lads in eye-glance contact
among some beautiful sirens
and food laid out like in a Renoir painting.

You sidestepped the jazz piano
wavered from the artist's way
for an arts job, much praised but often
derided as a fat-cat
Southside brat.

In the end you lost patience with writers
finding them always insecure and ultimately crazy
yet you kept faith for certain books

beyond the burn and permanent darkening
of the mind

That cough of yours
Bewleys, Georges Street '97
'Just a heavy cold', you said

What killed you, young enough at forty-eight
but too early for someone who boasted
of a well planned ripe old age?
The workaholic's endless toil as fix
Fundraising for Frankfurt in '96

Cancer encountered stolid bravery
you were indignant about giving into fear
steering my sadness at our last meeting
beyond an emotional scene. The farewell
heroic, old pal:
'I hope you and the likes of Mannix
get by alright, somehow.'

You went off in a blast of sunset
in the Coombe, not with your wife by the bedside
but your first love. Her hair more golden
in the last light of evening as she held your hand.
Death's radiant maiden leading you in the dance.

Pearse Station was heavily agnostic after the funeral
party. Cold steel tracks, rainy damp weather
and deadening sorrow.

Friend of youth's twenty years
Monkstown ghost
with wide-brimmed hat and flowing scarf.
What'll I do now, Lar?
Can I hear the shrouded face
reply: 'Keep you best side out
old son. Hang on 'till the end
and hope to get by, somehow.'

Paris

Tourists in the maze of streets
find the river but are stopped
by traffic on the *quais*
there was thunder earlier
muting the organ solo in Notre Dame
rain splashed the clocks of oysters
under the café canopies

grimy locked doorways
could be Père-Lachaise tombs
eternally overcoming fear
and laughing in the face of death

Latin-eyed commuters around Gare Saint-Lazare
pass Arman's tree of clocks
entitled *L'Heure de tous*

A beer is quenching
and gives energy to jostle for space
with the generative culture vultures

but who will stop the night
after a knife-edged day—
the funicular at Montmartre
ascends above the roofs
the extremities of cityscape
laid out in one vast field

sunset ebbs across a long vista
coupled with switched-on lights
what pleasures await the rising tide of people?

9/11

Fire is the sister of sunlight—
and in our time the Trojan horses flew

the angels of doom in aisle and cockpit
detonate two aircraft
like an explosive charge
in one tower and then another

these towers that fell
once formed the number eleven
on the skyline—

the crematory shrine
with a backdrop of girders
like two broken gates—
images on screen and photograph

the funeral rite in uniformed formality
grey and silver ash in buckets
passed from hand to hand
the thousands dead echoing in each leaf

the city was shaken
brothers and sisters a little cowed

someone picks up a child's battered doll
the city in a tremor with weak nerves
but they will strike back

for all of us can kill—
there is nothing different or new in that—

September 2001

When Myths Collide

Salomé always leads Herod a merry dance.
He, at eighty, is the proud father of eight adult-children
who loathe him—a fundamentalist Christian and sex-hater
who subconsciously fancies his oldest daughter.
The wife, Herodias—a withered wisp of a woman
with neuralgia, from the miserable marriage
to the mean Tetrarch, bald as a seal—
is also unable to let go. They live through their children.

'Salomé, you could do a lot better than John the Baptist,'
advises Herod, cautiously yet scared
of his daughter's independent rage and revengeful criticism
and the constant tongue lashing
for the way he still treats her mother.
It is a toxic saga but fairly typical
of that generation, who hold the family unit as sacred
beyond reproach and a model of perfection—
they could never admit family dysfunction.

Salomé has not only plumped for John—
the most unorthodox Baptist you've ever seen
more a cross with Lir, a divorced oddbod
with growing children, who in post-hangover
guilt, thinks he hears hungry seagulls wailing
and sensitive swans with ruffled feathers
hissing. He visits the offspring
wearing vagabond's gear and unkempt beard
as validity of his inability to pay maintenance.
His ex is no Deirdre of the Sorrows or Medea—
she flushes at the thought of how she could
ever have got involved with such a dose.

Meanwhile, John and Salomé live like Diarmuid with Grainne
closeted from the world, pay their rent and survive
wary of the gold rush. Grainne's grotto of a flat

has a Buddha that is missing one hand—legacy
   of sculpture class,
joss sticks, fruit and organic vegetables
but they are not far above the dole—
well-fed dogs bark at them as they drive to the sea
past lines of Mercedes and landrovers
in their yellow Ford Escort.

They look as if they are set up for further idyllic progress
with a tantric sex life, somewhat unsafe in their narrow bath.
They intend to go back to nature on an acre plot
build a wooden house, escape the city as lapsed hippies
in the Valhalla of the countryside, far from bungalow bliss
and holiday cottages, making their art products
commercial and if possible authentic.

Herod cannot make a stand against Salomé
at this late stage or she may dance
with Doc Martens on his grave.
Oddbod John's children are safer
with their hands-on loving mother than a wandering
father whose ambitions include a camper van
and a ceremonial union with Grainne, conducted
at a Temple of Isis somewhere in the mountains
by a woman who has a website invoking the return
of the priestess class to the length and breath of the land

This Mist, This Morning ...

I know that all night as we slept—
sure as nakedness and certain
of its stark beauty—
mother mist and father dew
were knitting and skitting
as they talked about their children

and this morning before we blinked
out of sleep, left their jewels
on grass and meadow, bush and leaf.
The tapestry of dawn has crochet,
lace, and tracery on spike and thorn—
these clothes are buttoned with berries

for the cluster oaks—
no-one except the secret God and the night
can make what is beautiful in the darkness
that we rarely see come to the light
of our dreamy and troubled eyes.

Witch of My World

Witch of my world
and witch of Plazac tonight
your breath and tongue
like mulled wine, hot and wet
banishing sorrow and fear

What can I do but follow you
away from the darlings of my fatherhood
the lost cause of my conscience
away from the peace I could not find

To survive for them, witch of Plazac
and you with a digital camera
flashing like falling stars
after midnight—
Ah how you frame the world.

Mary Pound de Rachewiltz

Fresh and unfussed you came from Brunnenberg
in the Alps, to lecture at Maynooth
for the Gerard Manley Hopkins Summer School
your father never owned a book of his poems
finding the metrical labours 'unduly touted'.

The theatre seated less than fifty and afterwards
you showed your translation of the *Cantos*
into Italian in a boxed edition.
A crowd huddled around, you smiled
and tucked up your head proudly
'And do they cohere?'

What about his years of incarceration?
'Ezra was,' (you admitted)
'a bad boy and had to pay
his debt to society.'
But the head shifted, the jaw turned on line
with your shoulder, as you signed
the bulky tome below your name
adding 'daughter - translator'

Then a lecturer said
'there was only one Ezra Pound'
and someone mumbled
'One was enough.'

These Words

two birds on those gateposts
that fly into the mind
with stone plumage
as they stand silent
Greek-eyed vacant
but
O their clay

And I could also write these words
in finger marks on the sand
then waves would come and
wash them away

Parnassus

Professor-poet invited
the Mexican poet, the Indian poet and the Jamaican poet
to his house for dinner
greeting them with
'The rumours of my being famous are greatly
exaggerated.'

Professor-poet's wife had also invited
neighbours, a he-poet and a she-poet
who brought along their baby daughter.
During dinner the Mexican poet announced
that he had two sons
　　　　　　　　who were
　　　　　　　　　　　fine young poets.

Professor-poet asked the she-poet
'Will your daughter be a poet when she grows up?'
She may well be, was the answer.
Later she asked him when he spoke of his two sons
'Do you think there will be a poet in either of them?'
He confidently replied,
'Probably in both.'

Homage To Thomas MacGreevy

Pound praised you in a letter
'promising' typed Ezra
Not in the cast of thousands
In those necropolyptic *Cantos*
Yesterday a slim volume of real poems
The surprise of some translations
All wrapped in acknowledgements annotations
and an introduction

The cool gallery lit by many a gem
A Poussin amongst them
Beside your portrait by O'Sullivan
The speakers at the launch
Tried to answer some questions
About the long silence on your part
Bound by the laws of Baudelaire
The Holy Spirit of Creation
The need to sign cheques
The civil servicing of Art

Afterwards at Toque Poussin
Someone remarked sadly:
'He went down with a touch of the Rimbaud's'
I pray to Tom who was a kind of saint
And a patriot.
The waitress spoke English badly
There was plenty of ice
Our coffee delayed
While old café songs of Paris were played
Would this city suffice?